PSYCHO SOMATIC THERAPY

A Complete Guide For Unraveling The Mind-Body Connection And Nurturing Mental Wellness For Physical Well-Being

WALTER ZYAIRE

No part of this book may be reproduced, stored in a retrieval system, or transmitted in any form or by any means, electronic, mechanical, photocopying, recording, or otherwise, without the express written permission of the author, with the exception of small extracts in critical reviews or articles.

DISCLAIMER

based on the author's research and understanding at the time of publishing, it could not reflect the most recent developments or practices in the treatment area. The publisher and the author both disclaim all liability for the accuracy, completeness, or use of the material in this book. Readers bear full responsibility for the decisions and actions they choose in light of the information presented in this book.

TABLE OF CONTENTS

ABOUT THE BOOK

A thorough manual that explores the complex interaction between the mind and body, "Psychosomatic Therapy: Understanding the Mind-Body Connection" provides insightful information for both professionals and anyone looking to improve their well-being. The book opens with a perceptive synopsis of psychosomatic therapy, detailing its goals and parameters as well as offering suggestions for efficiently navigating its contents.

Readers are introduced to the terminology, historical background, and basic tenets of psychosomatic therapy. The function of emotions in psychosomatic health is then methodically revealed, which also highlight the physiological effects of stress and the importance of emotional intelligence in therapeutic approaches.

The book examination of body-mind communication expands on our knowledge of psychosomatic symptoms and their significance.

It does this by providing examples and case studies from real-world situations that can be applied practically.

By looking at numerous psychosomatic techniques and therapies, such as body awareness, breathing exercises, mindfulness, meditation, and movement therapies like yoga and Tai Chi, the book keeps providing a well-rounded viewpoint. Holistic health and psychosomatic wellness are discussed, along with the critical roles that lifestyle, sleep, and diet play in attaining general well-being.

The examination of the therapeutic connection is a noteworthy high point of the book. The significance of developing rapport and trust, communication abilities, and ethical considerations in psychosomatic therapy are emphasized in this section. Case studies that demonstrate successful therapy outcomes are included to offer real-world application of these principles.

Useful methods and exercises are presented, providing readers with concrete measures to integrate progressive muscle relaxation, guided imagery, affirmations, and journaling for psychosomatic awareness into their daily lives. The book finishes by projecting future developments in psychosomatic therapy, such as discoveries in the field, the developing therapeutic approaches, and the use of technology in psychosomatic treatment.

"Psychosomatic Therapy: Understanding the Mind-Body Connection" is essentially a priceless tool for professionals and laypeople alike who want to learn more about psychosomatic health and develop holistic well-being. The book is an invaluable resource for everyone seeking to achieve their best physical and mental health since it skillfully combines theory with real-world applications.

CHAPTER ONE

OVERVIEW OF PSYCHOSOMATIC THERAPY

SYNOPSIS OF PSYCHOSOMATIC TREATMENT

A comprehensive approach to health and wellbeing, psychosomatic therapy examines the complex interactions that exist between the mind and body. This treatment approach is based on the knowledge that psychological variables have a major influence on physical health and vice versa.

Essentially, it acknowledges the close relationship that exists between our emotional and mental states and the physical manifestation of illnesses.

This introduction explores the essential elements of psychosomatic therapy, providing insight into its meaning, history, and guiding concepts.

COMPREHENDING PSYCHOSOMATIC TREATMENT

To comprehend psychosomatic therapy, one must acknowledge that the body and mind are essential parts of a single, cohesive system rather than two distinct entities. This method argues that a person's experiences, feelings, and ideas can have a significant impact on their physical health. On the other hand, physical health and physiological functions can have a reciprocal impact on mental and emotional health. Based on the idea that these two dimensions dynamically interact to determine an individual's total health, psychosomatic therapy emphasizes the significance of treating both for complete healing.

MEANING AND HISTORY

Psychosomatic therapy has its origins in several philosophical and cultural traditions that recognize the complex relationship between the mind and body. The idea of psychosomatic unity has been present throughout history, from mind-body dualism theories in Western philosophy to ancient Eastern therapies that combined mind-body approaches. Gaining an understanding of Psychosomatic Therapy's historical viewpoints might help one better understand how it has evolved and the various cultural factors that have impacted its tenets.

THE RELATIONSHIP BETWEEN THE MIND AND BODY

The Mind-Body Connection, which emphasizes the dynamic link between mental and physical processes, is the fundamental tenet of psychosomatic therapy. This relationship implies that our thoughts, feelings, and beliefs directly affect our physiological condition, affecting everything from organ function to immune system performance. On the other hand, physical health can have an impact on mental and emotional health. By utilizing this complex interaction for therapeutic ends, psychosomatic therapy seeks to advance balance and harmony in the individual.

The term "psychosomatic therapy" refers to a comprehensive approach that takes into account the individual as a whole, including their mind, body, and spirit. It acknowledges that diseases and their symptoms are not singular events but rather the outward expressions of more profound psychological and emotional processes. Psychosomatic Therapy aims to promote healing on several levels and a strong, long-lasting sense of well-being by exploring the underlying reasons and addressing the core concerns.

IMPORTANT IDEAS AND CONCEPTS

The foundation of Psychosomatic Therapy consists of fundamental ideas and concepts that direct practitioners in their approach to diagnosis and therapy. These ideas frequently include realizing that symptoms are symbolic, investigating how past events affect one's current health, and applying different therapy modalities to treat psychological as well as physical issues. These ideas' holistic orientation is consistent with the larger movement in favor of integrative and patient-centered approaches to health and well-being.

Psychosomatic Therapy is a fundamental paradigm that acknowledges the connection between the body and the mind. This therapy technique, with its historical foundations and modern implementation, aims to reveal the complex relationship between physical and psychological well-being. Psychosomatic Therapy provides a comprehensive framework for comprehending and supporting health by recognizing the Mind-Body Connection and upholding fundamental principles. It emphasizes the significance of a cohesive approach to healing.

CHAPTER TWO

EMOTIONS' SIGNIFICANCE FOR PSYCHOSOMATIC HEALTH

MENTAL AND PHYSICAL WELL-BEING

In the subject of psychosomatic health, the complicated interplay between emotions and physical health has attracted a lot of interest. Emotions, including happiness, sorrow, anger, and anxiety, are not limited to the domain of mental experiences alone; they have a significant impact on an individual's general state of well-being. Emotional well-being can either improve or worsen one's physical health, according to a scientific study that highlights the reciprocal relationship between emotional states and physical health outcomes.

STRESS'S EFFECTS ON THE BODY

One of the most important aspects of comprehending the relationship between emotions and psychosomatic health is stress, which is a common emotional reaction to a variety of life circumstances. Stress has wide-ranging physiological effects on the body, impacting everything from the immune system and cardiovascular system to the gastrointestinal tract. Prolonged psychological stress has been associated with ailments like immune system failure, digestive issues, and high blood pressure, indicating the significant influence that ongoing emotional stress can have on physical well-being. This complex interaction emphasizes how crucial it is to control and regulate emotions to maintain general well-being.

IN PSYCHOSOMATIC THERAPY, EMOTIONAL INTELLIGENCE

In psychosomatic therapy, the idea of emotional intelligence is essential because it provides a framework for comprehending and managing the complex interplay between emotions and physical health. Emotional intelligence encompasses the aptitude to identify, comprehend, and regulate one's feelings in addition to the ability to sense and impact the feelings of others. People with high emotional intelligence may be better able to address the psychological aspects causing physical health problems in the setting of psychosomatic therapy. Through the development of emotional resilience and adaptive coping mechanisms, therapeutic interventions that include concepts of emotional intelligence might improve the efficacy of psychosomatic treatment.

METHODS FOR MANAGING EMOTIONS

The creation and implementation of efficient emotion regulation strategies are critical in the field of psychosomatic health. By enabling people to control their emotional reactions, these strategies hope to lessen the detrimental effects on their physical well-being. Psychosomatic therapy utilizes many modalities such as mindfulness practices, cognitive-behavioral therapies, and relaxation techniques to facilitate emotion control. Through the development of emotional state awareness and the application of focused therapies, people can improve their ability to manage stressors and make good contributions to their psychosomatic health.

The complex interplay between emotions and psychosomatic health emphasizes the necessity of a comprehensive strategy that takes into account the reciprocal influence of mental and physical states. The dynamic interplay between stress, emotional intelligence, and efficient emotion regulation mechanisms presents important opportunities for knowledge and intervention in the goal of optimal psychosomatic well-being.

CHAPTER THREE

COMMUNICATION BETWEEN THE BODY AND MIND

THE BODY'S LANGUAGE

The human body is an amazing machine that communicates not only with other people but also with itself through a complex and silent system known as the body's language. Our bodies send forth subtle clues and signals that represent our feelings, ideas, and general state of well-being; this is known as non-verbal communication. Our bodies constantly communicate information about our internal states through posture and facial expressions. Gaining an understanding of this unspoken language might reveal important details about our emotional and mental states.

SIGNS OF PSYCHOSOMATIC DISORDERS AND WHAT THEY MEAN

The intriguing meeting point of the mind and body, where psychological issues materialize as physical illnesses, is represented by psychosomatic symptoms. These symptoms are a physical manifestation of underlying emotional or mental stress rather than just coincidence. Conditions like tension headaches, stomach problems, or skin illnesses are prime examples of the mind-body connection, as psychological variables either cause or worsen physical symptoms. A holistic approach to health must recognize and accept the psychosomatic nature of some illnesses since treating the underlying psychological causes of many conditions can result in notable improvements in physical health.

UNDERSTANDING PHYSICAL ILLNESSES

Physical illnesses are interpreted in a way that extends beyond traditional medical practice and into the psychosocial aspects of a person's life. Physical ailments are frequently messengers of unsaid feelings or unresolved problems. For instance, unresolved guilt or grief may be the cause of repeated respiratory problems, while persistent pain may be a symptom of suppressed grief.

Through the adoption of a more integrated perspective that takes into account the interaction between mental and physical health, patients and medical professionals can get a deeper comprehension of the underlying causes of different illnesses.

EXAMPLES & CASE STUDIES

Examining case studies and examples yields tangible representations of the complex interactions between the mind and body. Imagine a situation in which emotional trauma related to a previous incident is addressed to relieve chronic back pain, rather than relying solely on traditional medical interventions. On the other hand, reports of skin disorders becoming better after receiving psychotherapy emphasize the connection between mental health and physical health. These illustrations emphasize the value of a customized and all-encompassing approach to healthcare, taking into account the various ways that every person's body interacts with and communicates with the intricacies of their internal environment.

Body-mind communication is a complicated and multifaceted process whereby the body's language can be an effective means of comprehending the intricacies of the human experience. Through the identification of psychosomatic symptoms, holistic interpretation of physical diseases, and examination of real-world case studies, we can open the possibility of integrated health methods that address both the physical and psychological dimensions of well-being.

CHAPTER FOUR

PSYCHOSOMATIC METHODS AND TREATMENTS

MEDITATION AND MINDFULNESS

Both of these psychosomatic practices have received a lot of attention for their potential therapeutic effects. They are based on the cultivation of present-moment awareness and the nonjudgmental observation of thoughts, emotions, and physical sensations. They have their roots in ancient contemplative practices. This practice fosters a healthy relationship between the mind and body by helping people become more self-aware and accepting of who they are. Studies show that practicing mindfulness and meditation can significantly lower stress, anxiety, and symptoms related to a range of psychosomatic illnesses. These methods promote a greater awareness of the mind-body link, enabling people to better regulate their physical and mental well-being.

BREATHWORK AND BODY AWARENESS

These techniques are essential to psychosomatic therapies because they highlight the complex relationship that exists between breathing, emotions, and physical sensations. Consciously controlling breathing patterns to affect mental and physical conditions is known as breathwork. People can adjust their autonomic nervous system and promote relaxation and stress reduction by increasing their awareness of their breath. In contrast, body awareness entails paying attention to one's own body's feelings, motions, and positions. People can examine and relieve tension held in the body by combining breathwork and body awareness, which supports a comprehensive strategy for psychosomatic treatment.

BIOFEEDBACK TECHNIQUES

By monitoring and delivering real-time information regarding physiological processes, biofeedback techniques let people take control of their involuntary body functions. In addition to giving visual or aural input, sensors assess characteristics including skin temperature, muscle tension, and heart rate. By teaching people how to actively control these processes, this knowledge aids in stress reduction and self-regulation. Biofeedback's ability to promote psychosomatic well-being through improved mind-body awareness and control is demonstrated by the fact that it is frequently employed in the treatment of ailments like chronic pain, migraines, and anxiety disorders.

MOVEMENT THERAPIES: YOGA AND TAI CHI

To support psychosomatic health, movement therapies, such as Yoga and Tai Chi, incorporate physical postures, breath control, and mindfulness. Yoga, which has its roots in classical Indian philosophy, emphasizes the harmony of the body, mind, and soul. Asanas (physical postures), pranayama (breathwork), and meditation are used in this practice to promote mental clarity, strength, and flexibility.

With its roots in Chinese martial arts, tai chi uses deep breathing and gentle, flowing movements to improve balance and Qi (energy flow). By encouraging calmness, lowering tension, and enhancing general physical and mental resilience, yoga and tai chi both aid in psychosomatic recovery.

INTEGRATIVE MEDICINE AND PSYCHOSOMATIC HEALING

Integrative medicine is a comprehensive approach to healthcare that addresses a person's physical, emotional, and spiritual needs by fusing complementary and alternative therapies with traditional medical procedures. Integrative medicine offers a thorough approach to therapy by acknowledging the connection between the mind and body in the context of psychosomatic recovery. A mix of conventional medical treatments, nutritional counseling, psychotherapy, and complementary therapies like herbal medicine or acupuncture may be used for this.

CHAPTER FIVE

PSYCHOSOMATIC WELLNESS AND HOLISTIC HEALTH

THE EFFECTS OF DIET ON MENTAL HEALTH

There is no doubt that nutrition has a significant impact on mental health and that there is a clear correlation between our dietary habits and mental health. For the brain to work at its best, a balanced diet that includes important vitamins, minerals, and omega-3 fatty acids is necessary. Deficits in these components have been connected to cognitive decline, mood disorders, and even illnesses like anxiety and depression. A nutrient-dense diet that promotes brain health can make a big difference in a person's psychosomatic wellness.

PSYCHOSOMATIC BALANCE AND SLEEP

Sleep and psychosomatic balance have a complex and profound link. Both the body and the mind require restful sleep to regenerate and digest feelings and experiences. Sleep disorders, like insomnia or erratic sleep cycles, can cause mood swings, increased stress, and difficulties with cognition. Promoting psychosomatic balance requires placing a high priority on good sleep hygiene, which includes keeping a regular sleep pattern and setting up a comfortable sleeping environment.

LIFESTYLE ELEMENTS AND HEALTH

Lifestyle variables comprise a wide range of components, such as social connections, stress management, and physical activity, all of which add to an individual's overall state of well-being. Exercise regularly has been shown to release endorphins, which are the body's natural mood enhancers and help to promote mental well-being. Stressors can lessen their negative effects on the body and mind by using effective stress management strategies like mindfulness and meditation. Psychosomatic well-being is further enhanced by social connections and a robust support system, which are essential in preventing feelings of isolation and promoting a sense of belonging.

DEVELOPING A COMPREHENSIVE STRATEGY FOR HEALTH

To create a holistic approach to health, different facets of mental, emotional, and physical well-being must be integrated into a single, cohesive framework. This method stresses treating the full person rather than just treating specific symptoms and acknowledges the interconnectedness of various components. Alternative therapies including acupuncture, yoga, and meditation are frequently incorporated into holistic health practices as a complement to traditional medical treatments. A holistic approach looks at the lifestyle, emotional condition, and social context of the individual to develop a comprehensive plan that supports long-term health and psychosomatic equilibrium.

Obtaining psychosomatic wellness requires an awareness of and commitment to the interwoven ideas of diet, sleep, lifestyle variables, and the holistic approach to health. Understanding the complex interrelationships among these components enables people to take proactive steps to improve their physical, mental, and emotional health, resulting in a more holistic approach that supports a balanced and satisfying existence.

CHAPTER SIX

THE HEALING BOND

DEVELOPING TRUST AND RAPPORT

Building trust and rapport between the therapist and the client is the cornerstone of any therapeutic interaction. Sincere empathy, attentive listening, and a nonjudgmental mindset are the building blocks of trust. Establishing a secure and encouraging environment where clients feel at ease disclosing their ideas and feelings is essential to developing rapport. A strong therapeutic alliance is fostered by therapists who are sensitive to the unique needs and preferences of their clients and who understand the value of cultural sensitivity and respect for diversity.

COMMUNICATION SKILLS IN PSYCHOSOMATIC THERAPY

In psychosomatic therapy, clear and effective communication is essential for comprehending and treating the mind-body relationship. To read and understand tiny signs from their clients, therapists need to improve both their verbal and nonverbal communication abilities. Additionally, for client understanding and involvement, the capacity to communicate intricate psychological concepts understandably is essential. The therapy process is improved when the therapist and the client have a common language, which enables a deeper investigation of the psychosomatic variables affecting well-being.

ETHICAL ISSUES IN WORK

The foundation of responsible therapeutic work is ethical issues. Therapists are constrained by ethical standards that place a premium on informed consent, confidentiality, and the welfare of their clients. Therapists must avoid conflicts of interest, uphold professional boundaries, and protect their clients' autonomy and dignity. Cultural competency is another area where ethical considerations come into play.

They recognize the diversity of clients' backgrounds and worldviews while fostering an inclusive and courteous therapeutic setting.

CASE STUDIES IN THERAPEUTIC SUCCESS

Analyzing case studies offers important insights into how psychosomatic therapy is applied and what makes therapy successful. Good interventions, a solid therapeutic alliance, and the client's dedication to the therapy process frequently combine to produce successful outcomes. By examining these situations, therapists can improve their strategies, spot trends in client success, and gain insight from setbacks. Case studies further emphasize how customized psychosomatic therapy is, highlighting how crucial it is to modify therapies to fit the particular requirements and circumstances of each client.

The therapeutic alliance in psychosomatic treatment is a complex dynamic that includes developing rapport and trust, improving communication abilities, maintaining moral principles, and gaining knowledge from case studies. Psychosomatic therapy is more successful when it is approached with awareness and sensitivity to these ideas, which helps clients achieve their goals of holistic well-being.

CHAPTER SEVEN

USEFUL METHODS AND ACTIVITIES

GUIDED IMAGERY & VISUALIZATION

These effective methods involve conjuring up images in your mind to ease tension, encourage relaxation, and improve your general state of well-being. Through the use of all of their senses, participants in this exercise are taught to vividly visualize a serene and relaxing setting or scenario. By utilizing the mind's capacity to affect the body, this technique promotes calmness and relaxation. People who immerse themselves in pleasant mental imagery report feeling happier, less anxious, and more focused.

Progressive muscle relaxation, also known as PMR, is a stress-reduction method that entails methodically tensing and then relaxing various bodily muscle groups. With the use of this technique, people can increase their awareness of the bodily feelings connected to both muscle tension and relaxation.

A profound sense of physical and mental relaxation is encouraged by PMR, which involves purposefully tensing and relaxing muscles. It has been demonstrated that consistent PMR practice lowers tenseness in the muscles, eases stress, and improves mental health in general.

AFFIRMATIONS AND POSITIVE PSYCHOLOGY

People use affirmations, which are uplifting sentences they repeat to themselves, to develop a positive outlook and boost their self-esteem. Affirmations, which have their roots in positive psychology, seek to dispel negative ideas and swap them out for positive, uplifting ones. Affirmations can help develop resilience, self-worth, and a positive view of life when they are used consistently. Affirmations can be an effective strategy for fostering mental health and developing a positive outlook when included in everyday activities.

Writing down thoughts, feelings, and experiences in a journal is a contemplative exercise that promotes psychosomatic awareness. Journaling becomes a technique for investigating the relationship between feelings and physical health when it is utilized for psychosomatic awareness. People who keep a journal of their thoughts and feelings may learn more about how stress affects their body.

The ability to recognize patterns and triggers is made possible by this increased awareness, which opens the door for focused interventions that enhance both physical and mental health.

INCLUDING STRATEGIES IN DAILY LIFE

These strategies work best when they are included in everyday life. Finding times throughout the day to implement these activities can help with long-term well-being, but consistency is essential. This integration could include journaling every evening as a ritual, adding affirmations to morning rituals, and scheduling specific times for progressive muscle relaxation or guided imagery.

People can improve their self-awareness, proactively manage stress, and cultivate a resilient and upbeat mindset outside of practice sessions by incorporating these practices into their everyday lives.

CHAPTER EIGHT

PROSPECTIVE ASPECTS OF PSYCHOSOMATIC TREATMENT

PROGRESS IN THE FIELD OF RESEARCH

Promising advances in research to further our comprehension of the complex relationship between the mind and body are expected to have a significant impact on psychosomatic therapy in the future. Researchers may now investigate the brain mechanisms underlying psychosomatic diseases because of the development of sophisticated neuroimaging techniques like positron emission tomography (PET) and functional magnetic resonance imaging (fMRI). With the use of these technologies, one can see inside the brain and learn how psychological variables influence physiological reactions and vice versa. Interdisciplinary partnerships between psychologists, neuroscientists, and medical practitioners will probably proliferate as research methodologies advance, promoting a comprehensive approach to deciphering the intricacies of psychosomatic illnesses.

NEW THERAPIES IN DEVELOPMENT

Emerging methods in psychosomatic therapy have the potential to transform conventional treatment strategies. Mind-body therapies, such as biofeedback and mindfulness-based stress reduction (MBSR), have become popular because they can treat the psychological as well as the physiological components of psychosomatic diseases. Furthermore, a more somatic focus is being incorporated into narrative therapy and psychodynamic approaches, acknowledging the significance of the body in the therapeutic process.

Likely, models that take into account the connections between mental, emotional, and physical health—holistic and integrative approaches—will gain popularity. Including complementary therapies like yoga and acupuncture may also be a big part of building the therapeutic toolset for psychosomatic treatment.

USING TECHNOLOGY TO IMPROVE PSYCHOSOMATIC CARE

The potential for improving treatment outcomes and accessibility through the incorporation of technology into psychosomatic care is enormous. Virtual reality (VR), telehealth platforms, and mobile applications are increasingly being used as essential technologies to enable remote psychosomatic therapy, eliminate geographic obstacles, and broaden the accessibility of mental health care. Biosensor-equipped wearables provide therapists with real-time physiological marker monitoring, allowing them to collect important information about a patient's stress levels, sleep habits, and other pertinent parameters. Applications of artificial intelligence (AI) could help doctors analyze big data, spot trends, and tailor treatments to each patient's needs.